A WORLD

NUCLEAR DISASTER

Alex Woolf

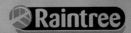

Raintree is an imprint of Capstone Global Library Limited, a company incorporated in England and Wales having its registered office at 7 Pilgrim Street, London, EC4V 6LB – Registered company number: 6695582

www.raintreepublishers.co.uk
myorders@raintreepublishers.co.uk

Edited by Andrew Farrow, Adrian Vigliano, and Vaarunika Dharmapala
Designed by Philippa Jenkins
Original illustrations © Capstone Global Library Limited 2013
Illustrated by HL Studios and Alvaro Fernandez Villa Advocate-Art pp4-5
Picture research by Mica Brancic
Printed and bound in China

ISBN 978 1 406 26093 9 (hardback)
17 16 15 14 13
10 9 8 7 6 5 4 3 2 1

ISBN 978 1 406 26098 4 (paperback)
18 17 16 15 14
10 9 8 7 6 5 4 3 2 1

British Library Cataloguing in Publication Data
Woolf, Alex.
A world after nuclear disaster.
§363.1'799-dc23
A full catalogue record for this book is available from the British Library.

Acknowledgements
We would like to thank the following for permission to reproduce photographs: Alamy pp 16 (© Aflo Co. Ltd./Mark Eite), 19 (© Michael Ventura), 30 (© Sebastian Plonka), 34 (© MARKA/eikon), 44 (© Troy GB images); Corbis pp 6 (© Roger Ressmeyer), 11 (Xinhua Press/© nhk), 12 (ZUMA Press/© Tepco), 20 (Sygma/© Thierry Orban), 22 (epa/© Everett Kennedy Brown), 24 (Sygma/© Igor Kostin), 31 (© Gabe Palmer), 33 (Sygma/© Anatoli Kliashchuk), 35 (Sygma/© Anatoli Kliashchuk), 37 (Sygma/© Igor Kostin), 40 (© Robert van Waarden/Aurora Photos/), 42 (Sygma/© Frederic Pitchal), 43 (© Reuters), 47 (© Andrew Aitchison/In Pictures); Getty Images pp 9 (The Asahi Shimbun), 10 (© 2011 Bloomberg/Timothy Fadek), 15 (AFP Photo/Go Takayama), 21 (AFP Photo/Ken Shimizu), 29 (Science Faction/Karen Kasmauski), 38 (Patrick Landmann), 39 (Barcroft Media/Zoltan Balogh).

Design features throughout courtesy of Shutterstock: empty cork memo board, background (© Reinhold Leitner), storm clouds (© KavardakovA), chain link fence (© ARENA Creative).

Cover photograph of a group of people in protective suits reproduced with permission of Shutterstock (© Leonid Shcheglov).

Every effort has been made to contact copyright holders of material reproduced in this book. Any omissions will be rectified in subsequent printings if notice is given to the publisher.

CONTENTS

Some words are printed in bold, **like this.** You can find out
what they mean by looking in the glossary.

THE ACCIDENT

The workers in our prologue are aware of the hazards of nuclear power – but what is nuclear power, and why can it be so dangerous? Nuclear power works by making use of the energy that exists inside **atoms**. It is created in a reactor. The atoms used in the reactor are from an element called uranium. The uranium is made into pellets that are put inside tubes called **fuel rods**. These are placed in the reactor inside a sealed chamber called the **core**.

Inside the fuel rods, a **neutron** (a particle within an atom) from a uranium atom smashes into the nucleus (core) of another, causing it to split. This releases other neutrons, which then smash into other atoms, causing *them* to split, and so on. This **chain reaction** is controlled by **control rods**, which absorb the neutrons being emitted by the fuel rods. By pushing the control rods into the reactor core, the reaction can be slowed down, preventing the reactor from getting too hot.

The fuel rods are immersed in water. The water absorbs heat from the fuel rods, preventing them from getting too hot. The heated water produces steam. The steam turns **turbines**, and the turbines generate electrical power.

With a nuclear bomb, the chain reaction is uncontrolled. The bomb releases an enormous amount of energy all at once, creating an explosion big enough to destroy a city.

Are nuclear reactors dangerous?

Most of the time, nuclear reactors are very safe. They have automatic systems in place to keep the fuel rods immersed in cold water and, if necessary, to shut down the reactor. Very occasionally, however, accidents occur and the core becomes overheated. When a core overheats, it can lead to an explosion, and the release of **radiation** into the environment (see panel below). Sometimes, molten nuclear fuel can melt through the vessel surrounding the reactor core and escape into the environment. This is called a **meltdown**.

WHAT IS RADIATION?

Radiation is the emission of energy, including light, sound, and radio waves. Most forms of radiation are harmless. The kind of radiation given off by nuclear reactions is dangerous because it is *ionizing* **radiation**. This is radiation with enough energy to strip atoms or **molecules** of their **electrons** (particles of an atom that orbit the nucleus). Atoms or molecules that lose (or gain) one or more electrons are called **ions**. Ions are often unstable and chemically reactive. They can react with chemicals in our bodies, causing damage.

We are exposed to a low level of background ionizing radiation all the time – it exists in the air and in the food we eat, and does not harm us. However, exposure to a large amount of ionizing radiation can harm the cells in our bodies, causing disease or death.

Earthquake!

The fictional state of Aramistan is a small, landlocked country in the South Caucasus, on the border between Asia and Europe. Aramistan has very little coal, oil, or natural gas. Most of its energy must be imported. The rest comes from **hydroelectric power** (energy from flowing water), and from its nuclear power plant at Rostemma.

On 1 May 2020, at 14.46 local time, a 6.5 magnitude earthquake strikes the Yerev region of Aramistan. Fortunately, this is a remote, mountainous area with few human settlements. The nearest big settlement is Rostemma City 60 kilometres (37 miles) to the south, which experiences some damage. Far more seriously, the earthquake hits the Rostemma Nuclear Power Plant, located some 10 kilometres (6 miles) north of the city.

In the plant's control room, the tremors are violent enough to knock technicians off their chairs and across the room. Alarms blare. The room is plunged into darkness – the quake has knocked out the plant's connection to the country's **power grid**.

Shutting down the reactor

A moment later, the lights come back on as the back-up battery-powered generators kick in. The chief officer gives the order to scram (quickly shut down) the reactor. In the reactor, all 20 control rods slide down through their guide tubes into the core, stopping any further nuclear reactions.

The control room is located in the plant's administrative building. Fifty metres (164 feet) from here stands the tall, dome-topped **containment building**, which houses the reactor. Maintenance engineers working near by are knocked to the ground by the quake. Above them, they hear a hissing and cracking as the pipe leading into the containment building starts to crack. Water spouts from the pipe in three great jets. This is the water that should be circulating over the fuel rods, keeping them cool.

HOW LIKELY IS IT?

How likely is a nuclear accident?

There have been six major reactor accidents in the history of nuclear power: Chalk River (Canada, 1952), Windscale (United Kingdom, 1957), Kyshtym (Russia, 1957), Three Mile Island (United States, 1979), Chernobyl (Ukraine, 1986), and Fukushima (Japan, 2011). However, hundreds of plants in 47 different countries have operated for many years without accident. Modern plants boast high-quality safety features, including emergency back-up generators and cooling systems, strong containment structures, and regular equipment testing.

This does not mean a nuclear accident can't happen. No safety system can deal with every kind of emergency. The environmental campaign group **Greenpeace** argue that just because there haven't been many accidents doesn't mean there won't be any in the future. Major nuclear accidents can be so devastating, just one is one too many.

The core starts to overheat

The containment building remains intact, but inside a serious situation is developing. Even though the control rods have stopped the **nuclear fission**, the reactor continues to produce heat. The burst pipe is preventing cooling water from reaching the core. As a result, the water surrounding the fuel rods starts to boil and evaporate, and the exposed fuel rods get even hotter. The fuel rods are made of zirconium alloy, which reacts with the steam to produce hydrogen. As pressure in the core builds, the steam and hydrogen is automatically vented into the reinforced-concrete containment building.

The chief officer in the control room orders maintenance engineers to fix the pipe as quickly as possible. Everyone is concerned that by the time the pipe is fixed and water starts flowing again, it might be too late: the fuel might have started melting through the bottom of the reactor vessel, and then through the floor of the containment building – in other words, meltdown!

Workers in the control room of a nuclear plant are monitoring the reactor. The equipment includes alarms to alert operators to any problems.

By 16.30, the pipe is fixed and water is flowing again into the core. No one knows yet whether the fuel has started melting.
At 17.14, the emergency battery runs out, and fire engines from Rostemma City are brought in to inject water from the river into the reactor's cooling system. By 21.06, mains electricity is restored to the plant, the pumps are switched back on, and the situation seems to be under control.

Rising pressure

Around this time, news of the disaster leaks to the local population, and with the help of Twitter and the blogosphere, the story quickly spreads around the rest of the country and the world. The Aramistani prime minister calls the plant director, demanding to know what is going on. The plant director informs her that there was a problem, but it has been dealt with. The plant is now safe.

A risky decision

Then, at 23.26, the chief officer is given some very bad news. A technician informs him that, due to the amount of steam vented into the containment building, the building has now exceeded its maximum operating pressure. At any moment it could leak, crack, or even explode.

The chief officer gives the order to open the valves in the containment building. This will vent some of the steam into the air, relieving the pressure. This decision carries risks: the vented steam will contain some **radioactive** material (material emitting ionizing radiation), which will be released into the atmosphere; the steam will also contain hydrogen, which might possibly react with oxygen in the atmosphere to cause an explosion – again, releasing radioactive particles into the atmosphere.

The chief officer is aware of the risk, but believes that opening the valves is still the best option available. He calculates that as long as the reactor itself remains intact, the radioactive material released will be small, and if there is an explosion, it is unlikely to be as big as the one that might occur if the pressure was simply left to build.

The valves are stuck

Unfortunately, when operators in the control room try opening the valves, they can't – the mechanism must have been damaged in the earthquake. The only solution is to send in some workers to manually open the valves. But the valve controls are located inside the containment building, which is now full of radiation.

The plant director asks the chief officer to choose three workers to open the valves. The workers take iodine tablets, which will flood their **thyroid glands** with iodine, preventing the radioactive form of iodine from being absorbed, potentially causing thyroid **cancer**. They dress in head-to-toe protective suits and face masks connected to air tanks.

These workers are placing spent fuel rods into a fuel pool. Fuel rods generate intense heat and radiation and must be kept under water for 10–20 years for safety.

Around the world, television stations interrupt their programmes to report news of a major accident in Aramistan.

At 00.14, the workers enter the containment building through an air lock. The atmosphere inside is dense with clouds of hot, white steam. Their handheld **dosimeters** (instruments that measure the body's radiation dosage) show very high radiation levels. Even in their suits, they are in severe danger. During the walk to the valves, they each receive over 100 mSv (millisieverts). The annual limit for workers at the plant is 50 mSv. The heat slows them down. Nevertheless, they manage to open the valves, then move as quickly as they can towards the building's exit.

Disaster

Radioactive steam pours out of vents in the building into the night air. A stray spark flashes, igniting the hydrogen. The resulting explosion blows the top off the containment building. The three workers inside are killed instantly. Outside, four more workers are killed and nineteen are injured. A giant cloud of radioactive particles pours into the air.

WHAT WOULD YOU DO?

Who would you choose?

As chief officer at the plant, how would you go about choosing workers to go in and manually turn on the valves, knowing the radiation may injure or kill them? Would you ask for volunteers? What if no one stepped forward? Would you ask the workers to draw lots? What if they refused? If you had to choose them yourself, what rules would you apply for the selection process?

MELTDOWN

Following the explosion, the shocked plant director offers his resignation to the prime minister, but the prime minister insists he stays, at least until the immediate crisis is over. When the smoke clears from the ruined containment building, technicians and engineers assess the damage. The good news is that the reactor itself was not breached. The bad news is that chunks of rubble sliced through electric cables connected to the pumps, and once again there is no water flowing into the core. Debris also ruptured several fire engine hoses that were drawing water from the river.

Fire engines spray water on the containment building in an effort to cool the reactor core.

Low Flow

The one remaining fire hose is hastily reconnected to the cooling system to try to keep the core from overheating. However, the single fire hose is not sufficient to cool the reactor core. Its flow rate is just 2 m³/h (cubic metres per hour), compared to 18 m³/h when the cooling system is operating normally. Boric acid, which absorbs neutrons, is added to the water in an effort to avoid a meltdown. Meanwhile, engineers work furiously to repair the broken power lines and restore power to the pumps.

Some radiation was released during the explosion, but not a devastating amount. Radiation dose rates at the plant increase to 101.5 mSv per hour. All staff directly involved in the operation to stabilize the plant, together with the firefighters, are issued with iodine tablets and full-body anti-radiation suits. All other staff are told to go home.

Government advice

The explosion is heard by residents of nearby Rostemma City. And this, combined with worrying reports on the internet, encourage many people to begin evacuating the city. A government announcement on all national television and radio channels calls for calm. The spokeswoman says that evacuation is not necessary, but as a precautionary measure, citizens of Rostemma and other nearby settlements are advised to stay indoors, turn off their air conditioners, and refrain from drinking tap water. If people must go outside, they should avoid exposing their skin and cover their faces with masks and wet towels.

FACT OR FICTION?

The nature of the beast

"We have to squeeze more electricity out of the turbine generator," [Victor] announced to the staff. "Otherwise, what do you think would happen if our steam supply would get cut off?"

"We'd lose power," one of the staff members volunteered.

"That's right … You know how important this is. The nuclear core needs water to keep it cool even if we're not producing any power. That's the nature of the beast. We have to generate enough electricity to keep the water circulation pumps going until we can bring the back-up diesel generators to full power. Otherwise we lose cooling water to the reactor and the *damn* thing blows up."

Excerpt from *Heart of the Monster*, a novel about the Chernobyl nuclear disaster, by Richard Opper (Amazon.com, 2010)

International response

As news of the accident at Rostemma filters into the global consciousness, nuclear experts are placed on alert. At 00.45 on 2 May, the Aramistani government officially notifies the International Atomic Energy Agency (IAEA) in Vienna that an accident has occurred at Rostemma nuclear plant.

The IAEA establishes dedicated communication lines with Aramistan. It informs all its member states of the news, as well as other international organizations, including the World Health Organization (WHO) and the Food and Agriculture Organization (FAO). The IAEA starts publishing regular updates on its website.

Meltdown begins

If the workers at the plant could see inside the reactor core, they would be very scared indeed. They would see that, despite their efforts, the meltdown has already begun. The fuel rods have been boiling away the water faster than it arrives. Left exposed for too long, the fuel rods have burst in the heat, releasing the uranium pellets, which have started to melt. The uranium has combined with zirconium and other elements of the core to become a molten sludge, known as **corium**. This super-hot, highly radioactive material is now oozing towards the bottom of the reactor vessel, where it has started melting through the vessel's steel floor. At 06.10 on 2 May, the corium eats through the base of the reactor vessel and begins to drip onto the thick, reinforced concrete floor of the containment building.

> *"We are on the brink. We are now facing the worst-case scenario ... If there is heavy melting inside the reactor, large amounts of radiation will most definitely be released."*
>
> Hiroaki Koide, a senior reactor engineering specialist, speaking of the situation at Fukushima, Japan, on 14 March 2011, three days into the crisis

Evacuation

During the course of the morning, dozens of people in Rostemma City fall ill, reporting headaches and metallic tastes in their mouths. Radiation levels of 0.15 mSv/h are recorded in the city centre, which experts regard as dangerously high. Normal levels are 0.0002 mSv/h.

At 14.00, nearly 24 hours after the accident began, the government orders the evacuation of the city, as well as all other settlements within a 30-kilometre (19-mile) radius of the nuclear power plant. Those who can are asked to go and stay with relatives. The rest are told to report to the railway station and designated bus stops from 16.00, from where they will be taken to temporary accommodation outside the exclusion zone. The public are assured that in a few days they will be able to return to their homes. As a result, they leave almost all their personal belongings behind.

Before leaving Rostemma City, evacuees are scanned with dosimeters to measure their exposure to ionising radiation.

A mood close to hysteria takes hold of the city. People stock up on supplies as they prepare to leave. The shops are emptied of bottled water, tinned food, batteries, and blankets. As the evacuees assemble, officials clad in white anti-radiation suits scan them with dosimeters. At 16.00, the first train, packed with evacuees, leaves Rostemma Station, and the buses start leaving the city in long convoys. Pregnant women and children are given priority. The convoy includes ambulances transporting the sick and injured, and secure police vans conveying the inhabitants of the city prison. The evacuees are taken to sports halls, schools, churches, and other large buildings in Aramistani towns and cities outside the exclusion zone.

Ghost town

By 02.00 hours on 3 May, all 65,000 residents of Rostemma City have been evacuated, as have the 15,000 residents of villages inside the exclusion zone. Rostemma City centre, normally thronged with people on Saturday evenings, is eerily silent and deserted, but for a few ghostly white-suited figures searching the streets for any stragglers.

Explosion!

Meanwhile, beneath the reactor, around 200,000 kilograms (440,900 pounds) of molten nuclear fuel is pooling and spreading across the floor of the containment building. Hotter than 2,600 degrees Celsius (4,712 degrees Fahrenheit), the corium starts burning through the building's concrete foundations, and then through the soil and rock beneath. At 02.32 on 3 May, the corium hits a large pool of **groundwater**, sparking a monumental steam explosion.

The second explosion at the plant is so powerful, it destroys other buildings on the site including the turbine hall.

CHERNOBYL

In the early hours of 26 April 1986, Reactor 4 at the nuclear power station in Chernobyl, Ukraine, went into total meltdown. The core exploded and radioactive smoke poured into the air. Firefighters arrived to put out the fire. They had no protective clothing and many became ill. The fire on the roof was put out, but the core continued to burn. A radioactive cloud drifted across the countryside. The local town of Pripyat was evacuated on 27 April. The cloud spread across much of northern Europe.

The explosion bursts up through the ground, destroying the reactor and what is left of the containment building. Steel and concrete debris flies through the plant, killing 28 workers instantly and injuring 52. The red-hot chunks of building material ignite fires in many parts of the site. The ground is littered with the dead and injured as an enormous cloud of radioactive steam pours out of the blackened shell of the containment building and gushes upwards into the sky.

Uncontrolled release of radiation

This second explosion is cataclysmic in its effects. The enormous cloud it produces contains particles from around 200 tonnes of highly radioactive material from the core, which are now being released freely into the atmosphere. The radioactive material includes uranium, as well as its **fission products** – atomic fragments that are left after a uranium atom has split. Fission products are unstable (they have too many neutrons) and therefore radioactive. The most harmful of these are radioactive **isotopes** (radioactive forms) of the elements iodine, caesium, and strontium. These are even more dangerous than uranium, as they can enter the food chain, poisoning humans and animals.

Over the next few days, winds carry the deadly cloud west across Aramistan and into Turkey. The cloud drifts across the entire Mediterranean area – southern Europe, the Middle East, and North Africa – before finally dispersing over the Atlantic Ocean. The accident at Rostemma has become an international disaster.

THE IMMEDIATE IMPACT

The two explosions and subsequent fires at the Rostemma Nuclear Power Plant have left a total of 35 dead and 71 injured. Six of the injured die later in hospital. A further 209 workers and 44 firefighters are hospitalized after suffering smoke inhalation, burns, or acute radiation syndrome (ARS). The symptoms of ARS are headaches, nausea, vomiting, stomach pain, skin reddening, hair loss, and a drop in the number of blood cells, leading to increased infection rates, bleeding, and **anaemia**.

Burying the problem

Following the second explosion, the plant director orders the complete evacuation of the plant. It is the last order he gives before being relieved of his post by the prime minister. Nuclear experts from the IAEA are placed in charge of the operation. They assemble a new team of firefighters, including a fleet of 20 helicopters. Their mission is not to save the reactor, but to bury it beneath so much material that it can no longer threaten the environment.

For the next six days, the reactor continues to burn and release its lethal gas. One of the jobs of the ground crew is to collect radioactive debris scattered around the site by the explosion, and to tip it back into what's left of the containment building. They wear heavy protective suits with lead vests. Even so, they can only spend a maximum of 40 seconds in the area around the containment building because of the extremely high levels of radiation there. Weighed down by their suits, they must fill their wheelbarrow, run towards the building, and tip out the debris – all in 40 seconds!

The helicopters drop a total of 5,000 tonnes of sand, lead, clay, and neutron-absorbing boron onto the burning heart of the reactor. The fire is finally extinguished by midday on 9 May. By then, the damage has been done.

THE FUKUSHIMA 50

The Fukushima 50 was the name given by the media to a brave group of workers who remained at the crippled Fukushima Nuclear Power Plant in Japan following the earthquake and tsunami on 11 March 2011. These 50 employees worked to stabilize the reactors after the other 750 workers had been evacuated. Four days later, they were joined by other workers, firefighters, and soldiers.

On 18 March, the Japanese prime minister said the workers were "prepared for death". By 24 March, 23 of the original 50 were injured, including several exposed to high radiation and suffering burns. All of them endured radiation levels well above safe limits, risking their future health.

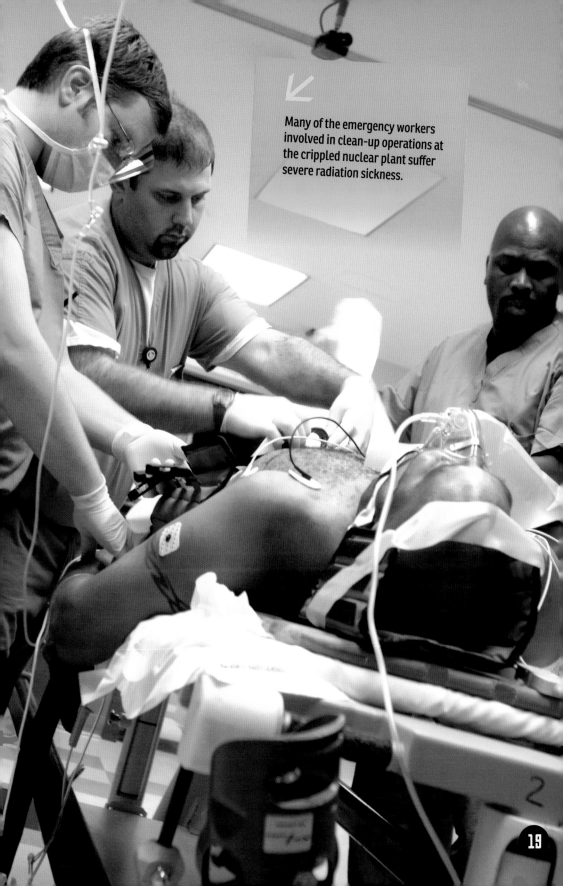

Many of the emergency workers involved in clean-up operations at the crippled nuclear plant suffer severe radiation sickness.

Criticism

In addition to the casualties at the plant, a further 42 local people, 34 of them from Rostemma City, fall ill with radiation sickness (though not ARS). Many media commentators blame the government for this, saying that evacuation should have commenced much sooner.

The government faces further criticism for its failure to supply many evacuees with adequate food and medical help during the first few days. The evacuation centres are poorly stocked and unprepared to handle such a volume of arrivals. Thousands of people arrive hungry, tired, and disoriented by their journey, and must go to bed on their first night without an evening meal.

Many evacuation centres are lacking in basic supplies.

"That morning no one suspected anything ... I'm preparing lunch when my husband comes back. "There's some sort of fire at the nuclear plant," he says ... I can still see the bright-crimson glow ... That evening everyone spilled out onto their balconies ... We didn't know that death could be so beautiful ... In the morning ... there were already military people on the streets in gas masks. When we saw them ... it calmed us down ... We didn't understand then that the peaceful atom could kill, that man is helpless before the laws of physics."

Nadezhda Petrovna Vygovskaya, evacuee from the town of Pripyat, near Chernobyl

A wider problem

During the days following the accident, IAEA officials armed with Geiger counters (devices for measuring radioactivity) fan out across Aramistan. On 6 May, they discover that samples of soil and water up to 90 kilometres (56 miles) from the plant contain significantly higher than normal amounts of the isotopes caesium-137, iodine-131, and strontium-90. This means that an area of 31,000 square kilometres (11,969 square miles) has been contaminated with radioactive elements that can get into the food chain, potentially affecting larger animals and humans. The area includes the country's capital, Hazgarok, and is home to around 300,000 people.

> *"In a few villages we measured the thyroid activity for adults and children. It was one hundred, sometimes two and three hundred times the allowable dosage. There was a woman in our group, a **radiologist**. She became hysterical when she saw that children were sitting in a sandbox and playing. We checked breast milk – it was radioactive … I knew that everything living should leave that place … But we conscientiously took our measurements…"*

Marat Filippovich Kokhanov, former chief engineer of the Institute for Nuclear Energy of the Belarusian Academy of Sciences, recalling a visit to the contaminated zone around Chernobyl

Following the accident, officials test animals for radioactive contamination, including people's pets.

Food ban

On 7 May, the government places an immediate ban on any food produced in this area since the accident. Farms are closed until further notice. Orders are sent out to all warehouses, storage facilities, processing plants, shops, and supermarkets in the country: any food received from the contaminated zone since 1 May must be immediately removed and destroyed. Government inspectors watch as large stocks of fresh fish, meat, vegetables, dairy products, and drinking water are disposed of. Representatives of farmers and others in the food industry call a meeting with the Health Minister. They demand compensation for their losses.

↗

Dairy products, including milk, cream, yogurt, and cheese, produced by farms close to the plant, are removed from supermarket shelves and destroyed.

Safety precautions

People living between 30 and 50 kilometres (19 and 31 miles) from the plant are advised to stay indoors, shut the windows, turn off their air conditioners, and avoid drinking tap water. They are also told to avoid any water drawn from wells because tests have shown that groundwater is contaminated. They are warned not to boil contaminated water: radioactive particles will then become airborne in the steam. If people must go out, they are advised to cover their bodies and wear face masks. Arrangements are made to evacuate any children and pregnant women from this wider zone. The government also announces that it is stockpiling iodine tablets and will shortly be offering them for free to anyone living within 90 kilometres (56 miles) of the plant.

This announcement causes great consternation among people living in this zone. Some voluntarily evacuate to more distant towns and cities, but most stay put. A great many don face masks, hats, and long, thick coats and converge on their local food shops. They quickly buy all the tinned and frozen foods and bottled water they can lay their hands on. No one goes out to work or school. The largest settlement in the zone is Arshavir (population: 15,000). The town's bank, its businesses, library, school, and most of its shops close.

The weather is warm, and many are forced to endure days of discomfort, stuck in their houses without air conditioning or fresh air. Government websites crash several times due to the sheer number of people logging on for any useful information. Many are confused by the conflicting advice they find on the internet about radiation and its effects. The Health Ministry offers evacuation to anyone exhibiting symptoms of ARS. Over 3,000 people call in to take up this offer. Most turn out to have nothing wrong with them. On 15 May, the government sets in motion the evacuation of this zone, which takes place over a period of two weeks.

The international impact

During the first 10 days, around 15,000 gigabecquerels (GBq) of radioactive material are released (a gigabecquerel is a unit of radioactivity). This is 500 times more radioactive material than was released by the atomic bomb dropped on Hiroshima, Japan. Over 150,000 square kilometres (57,915 square miles) of land are contaminated with **fallout** (radioactive particles).

Fallout is particularly intense in areas receiving rainfall from clouds that form above the radioactive cloud. Rome, Italy, is badly hit. High levels of radioactive contamination are recorded in the city's supplies of milk, cheese, pasta, pizza dough, vegetables, meat, and fish – in some cases 1,000 times above normal levels. There is a rise in doctor visits, with people complaining of nausea, fatigue, vomiting, and diarrhoea. The government bans all fresh foods grown and sold in the Lazio region.

Downturn

There follows a mass dumping of foodstuffs and a major downturn in business for Rome's many food outlets, cafes, and restaurants. The Rome Wine Festival, scheduled for May, is cancelled amid fears that some of the barrels have been contaminated.

Holidaymakers throughout the Mediterranean area return home early, causing massive queues and chaos at airports from Cairo to Majorca. Travel agencies report a dramatic drop in bookings for the summer.

Hotlines and radiation stations

Many of the affected countries set up hotlines, which are soon flooded with millions of anxious calls, demanding updates on local radiation levels and advice on what to do. After a scare in northern Greece, several towns are virtually abandoned in an unofficial, panicked evacuation.

Many fish in nearby lakes and rivers died from exposure to radiation. These ones grew unusually large and flabby, and jumped out of the lake before they died.

Across the Middle East and Europe, from Egypt to the United Kingdom, governments set up "radiation stations" in an effort to calm the fears of their jittery populations. The stations send real-time data on radiation levels, via satellite, to IAEA officials, who make the information available to the public online.

FISSION PRODUCTS

The most dangerous radioactive particles are the fission products – products created during nuclear fission. The three main fission products are the isotopes iodine-131, caesium-137, and strontium-90. All can be inhaled as particles in the air or absorbed through contaminated food and drink. Exposure to any of them can cause cancer.

Research centres produce sophisticated computer models to predict how radioactive releases from Rostemma could spread through the atmosphere.

Throughout the world, radiation experts move into the ports and airports, testing the people and products as they arrive. There is a minor panic at Heathrow Airport, when a businessman from Zagreb is taken ill with suspected radiation poisoning. Officials try to reassure fellow passengers that radiation sickness is not **contagious**. It emerges later that he was suffering from flu.

Boycott

A consignment of dried apricots from Turkey, arriving in Boston Harbor, USA, is found to contain high levels of caesium-137. Similar reports begin surfacing in many parts of the world, prompting a general boycott of foodstuffs from the affected areas. Under public pressure, governments impose bans on food imports from the Middle East, North Africa, and southern Europe. Sales of Mediterranean olives, citrus fruits, and grapes plummet, and it will be many years before these industries recover.

When can we go home?

When the evacuation was first announced, evacuees were told it would last no more than three days. The clean-up people would move in, wash everything, check it over, and then they could return. That was 11 days ago. Since then news reports have suggested that the contamination is worse than was first believed. Representatives of the evacuees press the health minister for an explanation. He admits that it may be three years before the area is safe enough for people to return to.

The evacuees are shocked to hear this. They have left most of their possessions in their homes. They were even forced to leave their pets, as radiation stays in animal fur and can't be cleaned. Suddenly, they are faced with the prospect of starting their lives again from scratch. They receive compensation money from the government. But for how long can they remain on state welfare? What will become of them in the long term?

Effects of the nuclear disaster

These maps show the fictional nuclear disaster in Aramistan, and how the effects spread across the Middle East, Europe, and Africa.

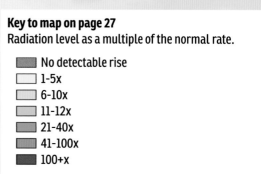

Key to map on page 27
Radiation level as a multiple of the normal rate.

- No detectable rise
- 1-5x
- 6-10x
- 11-12x
- 21-40x
- 41-100x
- 100+x

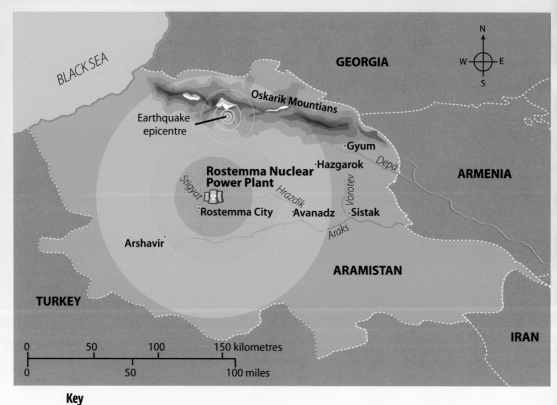

BLACK SEA

GEORGIA

N
W — E
S

Oskarik Mountians

Earthquake epicentre

Gyum

Hazgarok

Depa

ARMENIA

Rostemma Nuclear Power Plant

Stigyat

Hrazdik

Vorotev

Avanadz   Sistak

Rostemma City

Araks

Arshavir

ARAMISTAN

TURKEY

IRAN

0	50	100	150 kilometres
0	50		100 miles

Key

- 30 kilometre zone. Evacuated 2/5/20
- 50 kilometre zone. Evacuated 15/5/20
- 90 kilometre zone. Food ban instituted 7/5/20

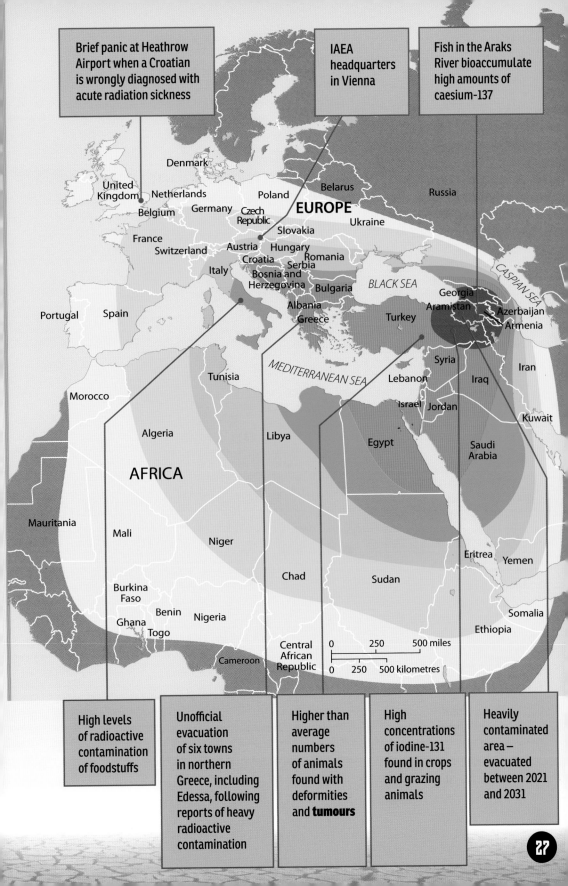

Brief panic at Heathrow Airport when a Croatian is wrongly diagnosed with acute radiation sickness

IAEA headquarters in Vienna

Fish in the Araks River bioaccumulate high amounts of caesium-137

Denmark

United Kingdom
Netherlands
Belgium
Germany
Poland
Belarus
Russia

EUROPE

Czech Republic
Ukraine

France
Switzerland
Austria
Slovakia
Hungary
Romania

Croatia
Serbia
Italy
Bosnia and Herzegovina
Bulgaria

BLACK SEA

Portugal
Spain
Albania
Greece
Turkey
Georgia
Aramistan
Azerbaijan
Armenia

CASPIAN SEA

Tunisia

MEDITERRANEAN SEA

Syria
Lebanon
Iraq
Iran

Morocco
Israel
Jordan
Kuwait

Algeria
Libya
Egypt
Saudi Arabia

AFRICA

Mauritania

Mali
Niger

Chad
Sudan
Eritrea
Yemen

Burkina Faso
Benin
Nigeria
Somalia

Ghana
Togo
Ethiopia

Cameroon
Central African Republic

| 0 | 250 | 500 miles |
| 0 | 250 | 500 kilometres |

High levels of radioactive contamination of foodstuffs

Unofficial evacuation of six towns in northern Greece, including Edessa, following reports of heavy radioactive contamination

Higher than average numbers of animals found with deformities and **tumours**

High concentrations of iodine-131 found in crops and grazing animals

Heavily contaminated area – evacuated between 2021 and 2031

Prejudice

The evacuees get on with their lives as best they can. Many of them – especially those showing symptoms of radiation sickness – suffer prejudice from people in the communities where they have been settled. A myth arises that radiation sickness is contagious. Some are barred from local shops and restaurants.

Children from Rostemma, when placed in local schools, are bullied or excluded by their classmates. They're called names like "Shiny" and "Rostemma Rabbit". The children push them into rooms with the lights off to see if they glow in the dark. Their parents fear even more for the future. They have heard that exposure to radiation can lead to cancer, and children with birth defects.

"The other day my daughter said to me: "Mom, if I give birth to a damaged child, I'm still going to love him." Can you imagine that? She's in the tenth grade, and she already has such thoughts … Some acquaintances of ours recently gave birth to a son, their first. They're a young, handsome pair. And their boy has a mouth that stretches to his ears and no ears. I don't visit them like I used to, but my daughter doesn't mind, she looks in on them all the time."

Nadezhda Afanasyevna Burakova, resident of Khoyniki in Belarus, which suffered heavy radioactive fallout from the Chernobyl accident

Energy shortages

The closure of the Rostemma Nuclear Plant has caused an energy crisis in Aramistan, a country lacking reserves of coal, oil, and natural gas. Aramistan has nine hydroelectric power plants placed along its fast-flowing rivers, but even at full capacity, these cannot provide more than 33 per cent of its electricity needs. The government therefore imposes a temporary system of energy rationing.

Electricity from the power grid is supplied for eight hours per day, from 08.00 to 12.00, and from 15.00 to 19.00. For the rest of the time, people must use candles and whatever local sources of power they can find. The government manages to negotiate with Russia for an increase in the supply of natural gas, but it is a month before electricity supplies are back to normal.

↘ Radiation victims must be decontaminated. Removing clothing and shoes eliminates around 90% of external contamination. Gentle washing with soap and water removes additional particles from the skin.

International aid

The Aramistani government is struggling to deal with the deepening social and economic problems created by the Rostemma disaster. The cost of the clean-up operation, rehousing the evacuees, and compensation payments to evacuees and food producers from the contaminated zone, is running to billions of dollars. Aramistan is a small country, lacking the financial resources to deal with a crisis of this magnitude.

Luckily, the international community has been generous. Since the accident, donations of money, food, blankets, children's toys, and medicine have poured in from abroad, both from governments and private individuals. The UN Office for the Coordination of Humanitarian Affairs (OCHA) has helped to manage this flow of emergency aid. The International Red Cross has worked with the Aramistani Health Ministry to set up mobile hospitals on the edges of the exclusion zone for the treatment of people with radiation sickness. Health professionals from Russia, Japan, and the United States, with experience of dealing with radiation sickness, have travelled to Aramistan to offer their services.

THE FALLOUT

As May turns to June, the people of Aramistan face an uncertain future. The fires may have been extinguished at the nuclear plant, but scientists are expressing anxiety about the molten fuel still burning away beneath the ground. And the radioactivity already released into the air and groundwater has contaminated thousands of square kilometres. What will the consequences be for those exposed to the radiation, and for any children they may have?

To prevent any further release of radiation from the plant, a giant sarcophagus is built over the remains of the containment building.

THE CHERNOBYL SARCOPHAGUS

The giant concrete sarcophagus, built in just 200 days in 1986 to contain Chernobyl's Reactor 4, is crumbling. A replacement is due to be completed by 2016. The frame alone will be made from 18,000 tonnes of steel, more than was used for the Eiffel Tower in Paris. It will be assembled several hundred metres from the site, to protect workers from radiation. The new sarcophagus will last only 100 years. Experts predict that the site of the reactor itself may not be truly safe for another 720,000 years.

↖

Construction
workers hired
to build the
sarcophagus
must dress from
head to toe in
protective anti-
radiation suits.

The sarcophagus

In early June 2020, an international panel of nuclear scientists call for the construction of a steel and concrete **sarcophagus** over the shattered containment building at Rostemma. They fear that there is still enough corium left after the explosion to start a self-sustaining nuclear chain reaction. If this is exposed to a large quantity of water, it could spark another explosion and a further release of radiation. They argue that a sarcophagus will seal off the corium from rain or groundwater.

Construction begins on 16 June and takes eight months. Over 250,000 construction workers and coal miners from all over the world work on the project, and they all reach their lifetime limits of radiation exposure. As construction progresses, the building becomes increasingly radioactive, until it is impossible to screw in nuts and bolts or apply welding, and this work must be completed by robots. The finished sarcophagus seals in around 750,000 cubic metres of radioactive debris, as well as the corium.

Decontamination

In February 2021, the government announces that the immediate crisis is over. Rostemma has now been stabilized. The sarcophagus has effectively sealed in the radiation. The core remains hot and extremely radioactive, but there is no longer any danger of another explosion. However, they admit that it will take decades rather than years to decontaminate the surrounding area. Not only must every single object be thoroughly cleansed with special chemicals, but the entire **topsoil** of the region will need to be scraped away, and trees near the plant must be buried in concrete pits.

The Dead Zone

Six hundred thousand **conscripts** have spent the past eight months engaged in a clean-up operation, and the job is barely begun. The government may not be able to afford the cost of the operation beyond the next few years. Most nuclear experts predict that if nature is left to finish the job, decontamination will take at least 100 years. They predict that Rostemma City and the other evacuated towns will effectively pass into history, no more than names on a map. In the media, the evacuated area acquires a bleak new name: the Dead Zone.

> "We had to remove the top layers of soil and load it up on trucks … We lifted out the topsoil in one big roll like a carpet with all the worms and bugs and spiders inside! But you can't skin the whole country; you can't take everything that lives in the earth. We stripped thousands of kilometres not just of earth but of orchards, houses, schools – everything."
>
> Igor, a former "liquidator" at Chernobyl, talks about his work

Continuing stigma

The Rostemma evacuees greet this news with despair. Nine months on, their lives remain tough. Most have been moved from the evacuation centres into government-owned housing. People who have spent their lives as farmers suddenly find themselves living in high-rise flats in the city. Now they must accept that they may have permanently lost the land that has belonged to their family, in some cases, for generations.

The stigma of being a Rostemma refugee remains as strong as ever. Local people resent their arrival and are envious of the flats that the government has built for them. To get a job, refugees must often lie about where they have come from. Young resettlers struggle to find a partner, as there is a fear that any child they produce will be deformed. As a result, most Rostemma refugees associate mainly with each other.

Some refugees are prepared to ignore the health warnings and return to their homes in the Dead Zone to retrieve precious belongings. They go at night, crossing fields and wading through rivers to avoid government checkpoints. Those who can afford to, bribe Dead Zone workers to recover their possessions.

Battles for compensation

Money remains a serious issue for many Rostemma refugees, especially those who, due to ill health or local prejudice, have failed to find work. When they were first evacuated, people were offered lump sums equivalent to around US$6,000, plus an additional US$2,000 per month – slightly more for pregnant women or families with children. However, in order to qualify for the lump sums, evacuees had to sign a form agreeing not to seek additional compensation later on.

> *"We are paying for food and utility expenses from my part-time job. We can't even pay rent. Out of goodwill, the current landlord says he won't demand rent until summer. But that will end soon. I don't know what we will do then."*

Mia Isogai, speaking a year after Fukushima. After the accident, she fled with her husband and two-year-old son to Yokohama.

↙

Many refugees from the contaminated zone have contracted thyroid cancer, including some children. The compensation they have received is often insufficient to cover their medical costs.

New evacuations

Eighteen months after the accident, the IAEA produces a new radiation map, showing areas of high radioactive contamination up to 1,000 kilometres (620 miles) from the plant. A new round of evacuations begins. Over the next 10 years, close to five million people are resettled from the most severely contaminated areas. In some cases, whole cities, such as Erzurum in Turkey (population 350,000), are permanently abandoned. This time the process is executed more gradually and with greater planning. Evacuees are given time and financial support to help them with the move. Nevertheless, it represents a massive upheaval for the people concerned, the break-up of hundreds of close-knit communities, and considerable economic cost and disruption.

> *"What happens during first contact with radiation is that your good **flora** is depleted and the bad flora starts to flourish. I suddenly wanted to sleep all the time and eat a lot ... They found [my thyroid tumour] during a routine medical inspection after I had worked there several years ... I had an operation to remove half the thyroid gland. The tumour grew back, and last year I had the other half removed. I live on [thyroid] **hormones** now."*
>
> Natalia Manzurova, who worked on the clean-up of Chernobyl

Life in an emergency camp comes to seem like a permanent form of existence for many refugees.

Health of Dead Zone workers

People were exposed to radiation from the Rostemma accident by breathing radioactive materials in the air, by touching radioactive materials on the ground, or by consuming radioactive materials in food and drink. Worst affected were the emergency workers who fought to stabilize the reactor in the immediate aftermath of the accident. A total of 252 were diagnosed with acute radiation syndrome (ARS), and 108 of them died over the following months. The next most at-risk groups were the construction workers and miners who built the sarcophagus, and the workers engaged in the Dead Zone clean-up. None of these contracted ARS, but up to 10,000 of them have suffered fatal cancers.

These are mutant apples growing near the contaminated site at Chernobyl, Ukraine.

Health of the general population

The worst effects of the radioactive cloud lie in a cone-shaped region extending west of Rostemma for around 1,500 kilometres (930 miles). This area has witnessed a dramatic increase in cancer rates.

The World Health Organization (WHO) has recorded 12,500 cases of thyroid cancer in children who were aged 14 and under when the disaster occurred.

There has also been a sharp increase in the number of children born with birth defects and **Down's syndrome** in the years following the disaster. Among survivors, many have suffered damage to their immune and **endocrine systems**, leading to accelerated ageing, heart and blood illnesses, and mental illnesses.

Death toll

The death toll from the disaster remains disputed. The IAEA put the total at 21,000 in its 2040 report. However, Greenpeace claim that as many as 450,000 people have died from cancer and other diseases as a direct result of Rostemma. The huge difference in figures is due to the difficulty of proving that cancer cases were caused by Rostemma and not by something else. Many of these "victims" and their families have fought for, but failed to receive, compensation. The legal arguments continue.

Effects on animals

Since the disaster, farm animals in the Dead Zone have been born with gross deformities, such as missing or extra limbs, missing eyes, or deformed skulls. Many wild animals in this area have stopped reproducing. Birds have been found with deformed tail feathers and beaks. Populations of insects and spiders have greatly declined – they live or lay their eggs in the top layer of soil, where much of the radiation settles. Within 1,500 kilometres (930 miles) of the plant, animals have been found with smaller brains, **albinism**, and tumours.

"You see, they knew, the bees I mean, they knew something was wrong, but we didn't. Not until it was too late. I remember that morning well. I went out into my kitchen garden as usual; it was a lovely spring day and so beautiful … But something was wrong … I couldn't hear the sounds of bees … I put on my mask as usual and started checking the hives. They were there alright, sitting in the hives, not making a sound. There was no buzzing. So strange their silence I thought … It was only when they came to take us away, three weeks later, that they told us there'd been an accident at the atomic station over there. You see, that is just 15 kilometres [9 miles] from our kitchen garden. It's no distance for that radiation to come over here. We didn't know that, but our bees did."

Andrei, a farmer from Khoiniki, Belarus, near Chernobyl

↖

This deformed calf was one of many malformed animals born in the years following the accident at Chernobyl, Ukraine in 1986. Most of these animals lived for only a few hours.

Effects on fish

The Rostemma Nuclear Plant is located next to the Stigyat River, which was greatly contaminated with caesium-137 during the meltdown. The Stigyat feeds into the Araks River, and from there into Turkey and Iran. The fish in these rivers have bioaccumulated large amounts of caesium-137 – in other words, all the plants and creatures below fish in the food chain have been contaminated by caesium-137, and so the isotope has become concentrated in the fish. This has not stopped people from fishing in the affected rivers.

Effects on farming

For the first two months after the accident, high concentrations of iodine-131 were found in crops and grazing animals, as well as the milk they produced, up to 300 kilometres (185 miles) from the plant. Fortunately, iodine-131 decays quickly. Since then, the main concern has been crop contamination by caesium-137 and strontium-90. The plants have absorbed these isotopes from the soil through their roots.

Worst-hit areas

In the worst-hit areas, where the land has been exposed to over 40 curies/square kilometre (a curie is equivalent to 37 gigabecquerels), agriculture has virtually ceased. In parts of Aramistan, Turkey, and Syria, where the land has been exposed to between 15 and 40 curies/square kilometre, government scientists have encouraged livestock farmers to switch to arable farming, as crops absorb less radiation than livestock. On land with less than 15 curies/square kilometre of radiation, farming has continued almost as normal.

The greater the distance from the plant, the less contamination there is. Yet, the controls on farmers are often much stricter. In Portugal, the most distant country to be affected by the Rostemma gas cloud, bans are imposed on the sale of meat from land contaminated with just 0.025 curie/square kilometre.

In summer, the wooded areas near Rostemma City are in danger of forest fires. When contaminated trees burn, radioactive particles are released with the smoke. These trees near Chernobyl have been chopped down as a precaution.

Effects on forests

The effects on forests have been far harsher than on agricultural land. This is because caesium-137 is continuously taken up and passed on by plants and animals in forests. As a result, forest foods such as mushrooms, berries, olives, and game contain the highest recorded levels of caesium-137 of any organism. Unlike agricultural crops, which have become gradually less contaminated over the years, contamination levels in forest foods have remained very high for two decades since the accident. This has caused birth defects in many birds and animals of the Mediterranean forests and woodlands.

Poison ivy is growing around one of the deserted buildings near the Chernobyl nuclear power plant. Unlike Rostemma, wildlife has returned to the wasteland around Chernobyl.

FACT OR FICTION?

Chernobyl molecules

"The first stops of the wandering witches' brew from Chernobyl were Poland and Scandinavia ... Before long, the winds took Chernobyl's gases south and east, to blanket most of the European continent ... Every one of us now has in our lungs a certain number of Chernobyl molecules ... We breathe in some of Chernobyl's last breath every day, and will go on doing so all our lives."

Excerpt from *Chernobyl: A Novel* by Frederik Pohl (Spectra, 1988)

Life in the Dead Zone?

What of Rostemma's Dead Zone? Will we see life there again? In the years that followed the Chernobyl disaster, the 30-kilometre (19-mile) exclusion witnessed a surprising revival of wildlife in its abandoned farms, forests, and towns. In the absence of humans, many species flourished. The same cannot be said for Rostemma. The radioactive contamination of the soil and groundwater during the meltdown was too great to allow a Chernobyl-style recovery. Twenty years after the disaster, the Dead Zone continues to live up to its name. One of the few exceptions is a type of black fungus, *Cryptococcus neoformans*, that actually thrives in a radioactive environment. Robots have retrieved samples of this fungus growing on the walls of the reactor core.

CAN NUCLEAR ENERGY BE MADE SAFE?

Accidents in the nuclear industry are actually pretty rare compared to other energy industries. The trouble is that when they strike, they tend to be far more devastating. As we've seen, they can ruin vast tracts of land for generations. They can cause fatal diseases, birth defects, and environmental catastrophe. Can we avoid the horrific scenario described in the previous chapters? Is an accident like the one that occurred at Rostemma inevitable, or can nuclear power one day be made safe? Before we try to answer that question, let's make a final trip to 2020, and look at how Rostemma might have affected the wider debate about energy during that time.

For decades, popular movements around the world have opposed nuclear power. These gained in strength following the Chernobyl and Fukushima disasters.

THREE MILE ISLAND, 1979

On 28 March 1979, disaster hit Three Mile Island nuclear power station in Pennsylvania, USA. The water that cooled the reactor accidentally drained out of the core. The core overheated and the fuel rods melted. The fuel rods became so hot they produced hydrogen, which leaked into the containment building. At 13.50, the hydrogen in the containment building exploded. For the next four days, operators struggled to gain control of the reactor. By 1 April, the danger was over. A small amount of radiation had leaked out, but no one had been killed or injured. Nevertheless, the Three Mile Island accident helped turn many Americans against nuclear power.

"No to nuclear!"

In many ways, the Rostemma disaster could not have come at a worse time. Since 2019, the world had been living in the era of "peak oil" – the period when rates of oil extraction have reached their maximum. From now on, Earth's diminishing reserves of oil will become harder and more expensive to extract. The industry is moving into terminal decline.

Many people had been hoping that by this time, **renewable energy** sources, such as solar power, would have been able to replace oil. Yet renewables are expensive and unreliable and will continue to be so until better technologies come along to harvest them. Before Rostemma, governments were coming to view nuclear energy as the ideal "stop-gap" fuel, a bridge between the old era of oil and the new era of solar, wind, and wave. Nuclear would plug the energy shortfall until renewables came of age. Across the world, governments were busy drawing up plans for a massive expansion of nuclear energy production.

Then Rostemma happened.

This one event has changed everything. Public opinion has now moved decisively against nuclear power, and governments have been forced to shelve their plans to build new nuclear plants. The question they're now facing is whether to upgrade their existing plants to make them safer, or close them down altogether. Most of the public are in favour of closing them down. Oil may be in decline and getting more expensive every year, but there's still plenty of it – not to mention coal and natural gas – and none of these fuels has ever caused a one-off disaster on the scale of Rostemma.

Arguments in favour of nuclear power

The nuclear industry remains statistically one of the safest. Far more people have died mining for coal or drilling for oil than working in a nuclear power plant. Unlike fossil fuels, nuclear power does not emit **greenhouse gases** or contribute to global warming. And Earth's uranium stocks are estimated to be sufficient for at least a century. Unlike renewables, nuclear energy is – for now, at least – plentiful and reliable.

These government inspectors are checking the turbine of a nuclear power plant in Penly, France. Today, the nuclear industry is subject to strict safety rules. These aim to ensure that in the event of an accident, the reactor permanently shuts down and radioactive material is not released.

Arguments against nuclear power

Twenty-five years since Chernobyl, the world is still dealing with the human and environmental consequences of that disaster. Nuclear power is, by its nature, dangerous, and despite claims of improvements in safety, many scientists say that another accident could happen at any time. Global warming itself may threaten the safety of nuclear power stations: many reactors are built on coastal sites, vulnerable to the impacts of sea level rises, including flooding and erosion.

Aside from the danger of accidents, the nuclear industry produces large amounts of radioactive waste (see panel below). The waste is buried deep underground, but no one can guarantee that, in time, this waste won't leak back into the environment, contaminating water supplies and the food chain. Also, the nuclear industry must transport this radioactive waste to the burial sites. If a nuclear waste train was targeted by terrorists, tens of thousands of people could be exposed to cancer-causing radiation.

↗ This baby girl is being checked for radiation poisoning in Tokaimura, Japan, following a leak at an uranium processing plant in 1999.

NUCLEAR WASTE

Around 97 per cent of the products of the nuclear fission reaction are recycled to produce additional energy. However, the remaining 3 per cent consists of highly radioactive waste that must be disposed of. At the moment, the only way of handling this waste is to seal it in radiation-absorbing containers and bury them deep underground, away from groundwater sources, so that the waste does not contaminate the water supply. However, the waste stays radioactive for thousands of years, and it is possible that, over long periods of time, radioactive elements could eventually leach out into the environment. There is also a risk that a lorry transporting waste from a nuclear power station or treatment plant to a burial site could have an accident, causing a leakage of radiation.

No solution

Anti-nuclear campaigners point out that nuclear power will not solve the energy gap, because it only produces electricity. Therefore, it only partly deals with our need for services such as hot water, central heating, and transport. They also argue that the nuclear industry is extremely expensive. The costs of building and operating nuclear power stations, mining and processing uranium, disposing of nuclear waste, and ultimately **decommissioning** nuclear plants, are – so they claim – far more than the equivalent costs for renewable energy.

Nuclear-powered submarines can travel much further than conventional submarines without the need to resurface. However, there have been at least 14 accidents involving nuclear submarines since 1961.

The *K-219*, a Soviet submarine powered by a nuclear reactor, was on patrol in the Atlantic Ocean. Just after 05.30 on 6 October 1986, there was an explosion in one of submarine's missile tubes. Three sailors were killed, and a fire began. The captain ordered that the nuclear reactor be shut down, but the heat had damaged the mechanism and the control rods could not be lowered into the reactor. One sailor, Sergei Preminin, entered the reactor chamber and managed to lower the control rods by hand. But the door to the chamber had twisted in the heat and he couldn't open it. Preminin died in the chamber. If the nuclear reactor had exploded, it would have sent a radioactive cloud across the east coast of the United States. Preminin became known as "the man who saved America".

Accidents will happen

So, let's return to the question we posed at the start of this chapter: can nuclear power ever be made safe? No one can plan for all eventualities, yet with each new disaster lessons are learned and applied and nuclear plants become, in theory, a little safer. But can a nuclear plant, however "safe", ever be proof against human error, for example, as happened with Chernobyl? Or can it ever be strong enough to withstand a major, once-in-a-century natural disaster like the one that overwhelmed Fukushima? And what about the next disaster? It probably won't be like either of those – it might come from a flood, a power blackout, or a terrorist attack. However it happens, we can be certain of one thing: it will surprise us.

In theory, you could build a nuclear plant that's strong and safe enough to withstand any and all eventualities, but the cost of doing so may be so high that it makes nuclear power generation too expensive for people to afford. Nuclear power will probably never be completely safe because it involves the processing of highly dangerous and unstable materials, and that always entails an element of risk. So then another question arises: if it can't be made safe, are we prepared to live with the dangers? And, if not, what are the alternatives?

Renewable energy

Many people believe the risks of nuclear power outweigh the benefits and support the development of renewable energies as an alternative. Most countries are actively investing in renewables, including hydroelectricity, biomass (energy from organic matter), geothermal power (energy from the internal heat of Earth), as well as solar, wind, and wave power. In 2010, around 13.9 per cent of global energy consumption came from renewable sources, compared to 5.5 per cent from nuclear power. The rest came from fossil fuels.

Nuclear fusion

There are also forms of energy that may be developed in the future, such as nuclear fusion. Unlike nuclear fission, in which atoms are split apart, with nuclear fusion, atoms are fused together, releasing energy in the process. It's the same process that powers the stars, including our Sun. One of the advantages of nuclear fusion is that there is no chance of an uncontrolled chain reaction or a meltdown.

Scientists are researching the possibilities of building a commercial nuclear fusion reactor, but they face big challenges. To get atoms to fuse requires extremely high temperatures (about six times hotter than the core of the Sun) and pressures. Scientists create these temperatures and pressures using intense magnetic fields, powerful lasers, or ion beams, and they have been able to fuse deuterium and tritium atoms. However, tritium is expensive to extract and the energy yield from these reactions is not very high. To make nuclear fusion commercial, scientists need to fuse deuterium with deuterium. Deuterium is easy to extract from seawater, and the energy yield of deuterium-deuterium reactions is much higher. But these reactions require higher temperatures, which are currently beyond the limits of technology.

WHAT WOULD YOU DO?

Energy question

As the new Energy Minister of Aramistan, in the wake of the Rostemma Disaster, you are faced with a dilemma. As a landlocked country with very little oil and coal, do you:

(a) decide to import oil and gas from nearby Russia, knowing that this will make your country vulnerable in any future dispute with that country, or do you

(b) rebuild the nuclear power plant believing that new technology and designs are safer?

Reducing energy use

Another way of reducing our reliance on nuclear energy – thereby decreasing the chances of another accident – is by using less energy. This is something that we as individuals can try to do as we go about our daily lives. For example, we can try to consume fewer goods and only buy new gadgets, such as phones and computers, when we really need them. We can unplug our phone chargers when they're finished charging; turn off televisions instead of leaving them on standby; set our thermostats a few degrees lower in the winter, and higher in the summer – wearing warmer or cooler clothes is much more energy-efficient; we could switch to energy-saving light bulbs – and remember to turn off the light when we leave the room. If everyone performed simple actions like these, global energy consumption would dramatically decrease.

Energy for now and the immediate future

It may be that one day we will be able to produce enough energy by other means to allow us to shut down the nuclear reactors for good. But for now, and most probably for the next few decades, we will continue to rely on nuclear power for a portion of our energy needs.

This schoolgirl is using a solar-powered lamp in her home. Many people believe solar energy could be a safe alternative to nuclear energy.

WRITE YOUR OWN STORY

Why not write your own story about a nuclear accident and what happens afterwards? It's a great subject for fiction because there are so many dramatic possibilities. You could certainly grab your readers' attention with descriptions of the accident and all the terrible disasters that would inevitably follow. But just because the subject matter is exciting, that doesn't mean your story is guaranteed to succeed. Writing fiction is a craft that needs to be worked at. Here are a few basic tips to get you started:

The accident

First, there's the accident itself. Was it caused by human error? If so, how does the person responsible feel about his or her mistake – particularly as the full scale of the disaster becomes apparent? This scenario will allow you to really expose a person's character, their strengths, and weaknesses.

Or was the accident caused by a natural disaster – a hurricane, say, or a flood? A spectacular disaster could inspire some very creative and dramatic descriptive writing.

Once the accident is in progress, you could have some tense and scary moments as the reactor moves towards meltdown. Will the desperate firefighting by the workers at the plant stop the meltdown? Probably not, if your story is to be a dramatic one!

Consequences

Your story could broaden out at this point to look at the consequences of the accident for ordinary people. It's probably best to focus on the experiences of a small set of characters – say a single family living near the nuclear plant. Try to imagine how scary it would be to be caught up in a situation like this. You can't see radiation – outside, it looks like an ordinary sunny day – but you know that if you go out there you risk illness, even death. Maybe one of your characters has come down with radiation sickness. How will his or her family get hold of medicine? Your main character will probably need to take a risk at some point – perhaps leave the house to get food or help.

Evacuation

Another area you might wish to explore in your story is the sadness and upheaval of evacuation – saying goodbye, perhaps, to a beloved pet; trying to decide what to take and what to leave. Once resettled in a new town, your character will have to deal with the daunting prospects of starting a new school or finding a job, and making new friends. He or she may have to deal with prejudice or fear from the locals. These are all potentially interesting themes that will keep your readers gripped.

Plot

Finally, you need to think about the plot. What actually happens in your story? You don't have to be too detailed at this stage. But you do need to work out the basic sequence of events, including the ending. When plotting, it's worth thinking about dramatic tension – how will you keep your readers turning the pages?

Research

In order to make your story more authentic, it's worth reading memoirs and accounts of other survivors of nuclear accidents. Learn about their experiences, then try to imagine how your character would cope in similar circumstances. It's also worth reading about how nuclear reactors work, so you get the technical details right.

That's about it for your preparation. Now you just have to get started. Good luck!

TIMELINE

1 May 2020

14.46

An earthquake hits Aramistan, damaging the cooling system of the nuclear power plant at Rostemma. The plant briefly loses power before battery-powered generators come on. The chief officer gives the order to shut down the reactor.

14.50

The chief officer is informed that a pipe has burst and no water is getting to the reactor

16.30

The pipe is fixed and water recommences cooling the reactor

17.14

Emergency batteries run out and the pumps stop working. Fire engines are called in to inject water into the core.

21.06

Mains electricity is restored to the plant. The pumps start working.

23.26

The chief officer is informed that steam pressure in the containment building has reached dangerous levels. The valves to vent the steam are stuck.

2 May 2020

00.17

After the valves are opened manually, hydrogen in the steam ignites in the air, causing an explosion that partially destroys the containment building. Four people are killed and 19 injured. A radioactive cloud pours into the air. The plant once again loses power.

03.26

Power is restored and the pumps start working

06.10

Corium eats through the base of the reactor vessel and drips onto the floor of the containment building

07.44

Radiation levels are so high at the reactor that the plant director orders the evacuation of the site

14.00

The government orders the evacuation of all settlements within 30 kilometres (19 miles) of the plant

3 May 2020

02.32

The corium melts through the containment building floor and the earth beneath, hitting groundwater and causing a massive explosion. The reactor and containment building are destroyed, 28 workers are killed, and 52 injured. An enormous cloud of radioactive gas rises into the sky.

3-9 May 2020

Firefighters and helicopter pilots battle to put out the reactor fire. The radioactive cloud spreads right across southern Europe, the Middle East, and North Africa, contaminating vast swathes of land.

6-7 May 2020

Soil and water samples up to 90 kilometres (56 miles) from the plant are found to be contaminated with radioactive isotopes. The government places a ban on all food produced in this area since the accident. People living 30–50 kilometres (19–31 miles) from the plant are told to stay indoors.

8 May 2020

Rostemma is declared a Level 7 nuclear accident

12 May 2020

The government admits that it may be three years before the contaminated zone is safe to return to

13 May 2020 - 12 July 2024

A large-scale operation is embarked upon to decontaminate Rostemma's "Dead Zone". The job, involving half a million workers, is never completed due to lack of government funds.

14 May - 15 June 2020

Energy rationing in force in Aramistan

15 May - 30 May 2020

People living between 30 and 50 kilometres (19 and 31 miles) from the plant are evacuated

16 June 2020 - 12 February 2021

A sarcophagus is built around Rostemma's reactor to seal in the radiation and prevent another explosion

1 November 2021

A new radiation map is produced, showing areas of high radioactive contamination up to 1,000 kilometres (620 miles) from the plant. A third round of evacuations begins.

2021 - 2031

During this period, almost five million people living in contaminated areas are resettled

GLOSSARY

albinism condition in which a person or animal lacks natural colouring, called pigment, in the skin and hair (making them white) and the eyes (typically making them pink)

anaemia condition marked by a lack of sufficient red blood cells, causing pale skin and tiredness

atom basic unit of a chemical element

cancer disease in which cells grow uncontrollably, forming malignant tumours (tumours that get progressively worse) and can lead to death if not treated

chain reaction self-sustaining nuclear reaction: a uranium atom splits, releasing energy, which causes another atom to split, and so on

conscript person enlisted to perform a job

contagious likely to spread to and infect others

containment building steel or reinforced concrete structure enclosing a nuclear reactor. It is designed, in an emergency, to prevent radiation from escaping into the air.

control rod rod made of chemical elements that can absorb neutrons without fissioning

core central part of a nuclear reactor, which contains the nuclear fuel

corium highly radioactive, lava-like mixture of molten nuclear fuel and other parts of the core, formed during a meltdown

decommissioning dismantling a nuclear power plant. This is a complex and expensive task, involving the demolition of the buildings and the decontamination of the site, so that there is no risk to the public of exposure to radiation.

dosimeter device used to measure the amount of ionizing radiation a person, animal, or plant has absorbed

Down's syndrome disorder affecting people from birth, caused by a defect in the chromosomes (threadlike structures within each of our cells). People with Down's syndrome tend to have learning difficulties and may have heart defects.

electron particle of an atom with a negative electric charge

endocrine system system of glands in the body. Glands are organs that secrete chemical substances called hormones into the blood in order to regulate the body.

fallout radioactive particles that are carried into the atmosphere after a nuclear explosion or accident, and gradually fall back to Earth as dust or in the rain

fission product atomic fragments that are left after the nucleus of an atom fissions

flora bacteria that exists inside a human or animal

fuel rod rods containing pellets of nuclear fuel, used in nuclear reactors

greenhouse gases gases such as carbon dioxide that contribute to global warming by trapping the Sun's heat in the atmosphere

Greenpeace international organization that campaigns for the conservation of the environment

groundwater water held under the ground in the soil or in rock crevices

hormone chemical released by a cell or gland that sends out messages to other cells in the body. Hormones regulate functions such as digestion, growth, and mood.

hydroelectric power generation of electricity using flowing water to drive a turbine that powers a generator

ion atom or molecule that has been made unstable and reactive due to the loss or gain of one or more electrons

ionizing radiation type of radiation consisting of particles, such as X-rays or gamma rays, with enough energy to cause ionization (strip atoms or molecules of their electrons)

isotope form of an element made of atoms with a different number of neutrons than is typical for that element. Some isotopes are unstable and therefore reactive. This instability can lead the isotope to decay, turning its atoms into radioactive particles.

meltdown accident in a nuclear reactor in which the fuel overheats and melts the core

molecule group of atoms bonded together

neutron particle found in all atoms except hydrogen

nuclear fission nuclear reaction in which the nucleus of an atom splits on impact with another particle, causing a release of energy

power grid network of electric power lines linking a country's power stations to its electrical substations in order to transmit electricity throughout the country

radiation emission of energy in the form of waves or moving particles. Radiation can include heat, light, sound, and electricity.

radioactive emitting ionizing radiation or particles

radiologist medical scientist who uses X-rays and other high-energy radiation to diagnose and treat disease

renewable energy source of energy, such as water, wind, or solar power, that can never be used up. This contrasts with non-renewable energy sources, such as coal, oil, natural gas, and uranium (for nuclear energy).

sarcophagus traditionally, a sarcophagus means a stone coffin. Since the Chernobyl nuclear accident, it has also come to mean a concrete structure erected to seal off the radioactive remains of a nuclear reactor following a meltdown.

thyroid gland one of the largest glands in the endocrine system and found in the neck. It secretes thyroid hormones, which control how quickly the body uses energy and makes proteins, and also how sensitive the body is to other hormones.

topsoil top layer of soil

tumour swelling of a part of the body caused by abnormal growth of tissue cells. Tumours can be benign (they don't progress to anything worse) or malignant (*see* cancer).

turbine wheel or rotor that is made to revolve by a fast-moving flow of water, steam, gas, air, or other fluid, in order to produce electric power

FIND OUT MORE

Non-fiction

Nuclear Accident (Emergency!) by Angela Royston (Franklin Watts, 2011)

Fiction

The following novels focus on life after a nuclear war rather than a nuclear accident. They all deal with the challenge of coping with radioactive fallout.

Brother in the Land, Robert Swindells (First published: 1984; New edition: Puffin, 1994)

Children of the Dust, Louise Lawrence (First published: 1985; New edition: Red Fox, 2002)

Z for Zachariah, Robert C. O'Brien (First published: 1974; New edition: Puffin, 1998)

Websites

www.greenpeace.org.uk/nuclear/problems
The case against nuclear power is explained on the Greenpeace website.

spectrum.ieee.org/tech-talk/energy/nuclear/explainer-what-went-wrong-in-japans-nuclear-reactors
This website offers a clear explanation of the Fukushima nuclear disaster.

www.whatisnuclear.com/articles/nucenergy.html
This website explains what nuclear energy is, and includes some helpful animations.

www.world-nuclear.org
The World Nuclear Association is an organization that supports and promotes the nuclear industry.

Films

The China Syndrome (1979, PG certificate, 122 minutes)
This thriller about an accident at a nuclear plant is entertaining, but not very accurate about what happens during a nuclear meltdown. It tells the story of a journalist who discovers safety cover-ups at a nuclear plant outside Los Angeles in the United States.

WarGames (1983, PG certificate, 108 minutes)
A teenager obsessed with computers and video games hacks into the defence system of the United States by mistake. He accidentally brings the world to the edge of nuclear war and must now fight to prevent the ultimate disaster.

Topics to research

1. Research the 1957 accident at Windscale in the United Kingdom, one of the world's first nuclear accidents. What went wrong? Do you think an accident like that could happen today? Go to http://news.bbc.co.uk/1/hi/7030281.stm to begin your research.

2. Imagine there has been an accident at a nuclear plant in your city. You and your team are responsible for shutting down the reactor and preventing the release of radioactive materials. What are the main dangers, and how would you deal with them?

3. Research what has happened to the people living near the Fukushima nuclear power plant since the accident in 2011. How have they coped with evacuation, sickness, and bereavement? Did the authorities manage the situation well? What lessons can be learned for the future?

INDEX